COOL MACHINES

TEN TRUCKS

Chris Oxlade

W
FRANKLIN WATTS
LONDON·SYDNEY

Franklin Watts
First published in Great Britain in 2017 by The Watts Publishing Group

Credits
Series Editor: Amy Pimperton
Series Designer: Mo Choy Design Ltd.
Picture Researcher: Diana Morris
Picture credits: AM General: 20, 27cl, 31b. Belaz.by: 17t, 17b. Bondgrunge/Shutterstock: front cover main & clb, 1. CIFA S.p.a: 14, 15, 26b, 30. All images © DAF Trucks N.V. Eindhoven. All Rights Reserved: 22, 23t, 23c, 27cr. ESO/NOAJ/NRAO: 12, 26cl. ESO/S. Rossi: 13. FNSS Savunma Sistemieri A.S: 10, 11t, 11b, 26cr. Anton Foltin/Shutterstock: front cover tl & bra. Sanit Fuangnakhon/Shutterstock: front cover bl. Bogdan Hoda/Shutterstock: front cover cl. Kenworth. PACCAR Inc: 8, 9t, 9b, 26tl. Art Konovolov/Shutterstock: front cover crb & br. Vitaly Krivosheev/Shutterstock: front cover c. Liebherr-Werk Ehingen GmbH: 4,18, 19t, 19b, 27tr. Melis/Shutterstock: 7b. Miramar: 24, 27b, 31c. Natursports/Dreamstime: front cover cr. Natursports/Shutterstock: 7t. Pixel 4 Images/Shutterstock: front cover bla. Staff Sergeant Aubrey Rundle/US Army: 21b. Shockwave: 5, 25. StockPhotosLV/Shutterstock: front cover tc &tr. MC3 James Turner/US Navy: 21t. Wikipedia Commons: 2, 6, 26tr, 29t.
Leit Wolf/Shutterstock: 16, 27tl.
Every attempt has been made to clear copyright. Should there be any inadvertent omission please apply to the publisher for rectification.

HB ISBN   978 1 4451 5512 8
PB ISBN 978 1 4451 5513 5

Printed in China

Franklin Watts
An imprint of
Hachette Children's Group
Part of The Watts Publishing Group
Carmelite House
50 Victoria Embankment
London EC4Y 0DZ

An Hachette UK Company
www.hachette.co.uk

www.franklinwatts.co.uk

Note to parents and teachers: Every effort has been made by the Publishers to ensure that the websites in this book are suitable for children, that they are of the highest educational value, and that they contain no inappropriate or offensive material. However, because of the nature of the Internet, it is impossible to guarantee that the contents of these sites will not be altered. We strongly advise that Internet access is supervised by a responsible adult.

FSC
www.fsc.org
MIX
Paper from
responsible sources
FSC® C104740

CONTENTS

Words in **bold** can be found in the glossary on pages 30-31.

COOL TRUCKS!

Here are ten of the coolest trucks you'll ever see. But they're not just cool to look at. They're also cool because they are super-tall, super-fast or super-heavy!

Mobile crane – see pages 18–19.

Some trucks carry stuff. Sleek trucks deliver goods along highways and tough trucks work in **quarries** and on building sites. Some trucks do special jobs — mixing **concrete** and even transforming into bridges. Other trucks are built just for fun. They are used for racing and doing crazy stunts.

Look for the Fantastic 5 panel for each truck. Here you'll find out five great facts about the vehicle.

FANTASTIC 5

Jet truck – see pages 24–25.

MONSTROUS

Take a pick-up truck, add some massive tyres and you have a MONSTER TRUCK! Now you can perform huge jumps and other tricks.

Thousands of people come to watch monster trucks squashing old cars and jumping off dirt ramps. As well as huge wheels, a monster truck has a very strong **suspension** and a very powerful engine.
This truck is called *BIGFOOT*.

FANTASTIC

SUMMIT RACING EQUIPMENT BIGFOOT

- ⚙️ **Length:** 6 metres
- ⚙️ **Weight:** 5 tonnes
- ⚙️ **Engine capacity:** 9.3 litres
- ⚙️ **Tyre size:** 1.7 metres
- ⚙️ **Longest jump:** 65 metres

BOUNCE!
The suspension is very strong and super-bouncy so that the truck can land safely after a monster jump.

BIG WHEELS
Monster truck wheels stand over 1.6 m high and are made of super-tough rubber.

SHINY

With the Sun glinting off its beautiful metal body, a 'BIG RIG' thunders past. It's the ultimate truck for keen truck drivers!

This classic US truck has a long nose with the engine underneath, a driver's **cab** behind it and behind that, a comfortable rest and sleeping compartment. This truck is designed for tackling long-distance routes, pulling all sorts of different trailers behind it. This 'big rig' is a *KENWORTH W900L STUDIO SLEEPER.*

SOFT SEAT

The driver's life on the road is made easy with a comfortable seat, lots of **gears** to choose from, **power steering** and plenty of electronic gadgets.

LUXURIOUS

Inside the sleeping compartment there's a fold-out bunk, a table, a microwave oven, a television and a fridge.

FANTASTIC

5

KENWORTH W900L STUDIO SLEEPER

⚙ **Overall length:** 8.8 metres

⚙ **Engine size:** 9 to 16 litres

⚙ **Number of gears:** 10 to 18

⚙ **Sleeping compartment length:** 2.2 metres

⚙ **Number of wheels:** 10

FLOATING

Is it a truck? Is it a boat? Is it a bridge? This extraordinary machine is all three! The truck can transform itself into a floating bridge or a ferry.

Armies must sometimes get their troops, trucks and tanks across deep rivers, where there's no bridge, or the bridge has been destroyed. An **AMPHIBIOUS** BRIDGE TRUCK is driven to the water's edge, where its sides can be unfolded to create a bridge or a ferry. This particular model is called an *Armoured Amphibious Assault Bridge (AAAB)*.

FANTASTIC

5

ARMOURED AMPHIBIOUS ASSAULT BRIDGE (AAAB)

- ⚙ **Length:** 13 metres
- ⚙ **Weight:** 36 tonnes
- ⚙ **Top speed on land:** 50 kilometres per hour
- ⚙ **Top speed on water:** 10 kilometres per hour
- ⚙ **Produced for:** Turkish **military**

LINKING UP
Two or more trucks can be connected up to create a bridge long enough to cross a wide river.

OVER WATER
The truck has two water jets that propel it across the water when it's working as a ferry.

SLOW

This 28-wheeled giant carries delicate telescope dishes slowly but surely to the top of a mountain. Then it lowers them gently to the ground.

The 100-tonne telescope dishes this truck carries are part of the Alma telescope array. The truck, called an *ALMA TRANSPORTER*, hauls the dishes up to 5,000 metres above sea level in the Andes Mountains in South America. There are two identical trucks, named Otto and Lore.

REMOTE CONTROL
The trucks can be loaded, unloaded and driven by remote control.

ALMA TRANSPORTER
- **Length:** 20 metres
- **Width:** 10 metres
- **Weight:** 130 tonnes
- **Power:** Twin diesel engines
- **Top speed:** 20 kilometres per hour

RAMPING UP
To pick up a telescope dish, the truck drives up to it and pulls it up two on-board ramps.

HEAVY

This is a **HYBRID** CONCRETE MIXER, powered by batteries as well as a diesel engine. The batteries work an electric motor that turns the drum full of heavy, sloppy concrete.

A concrete mixer mixes and delivers concrete at the same time. The ingredients of the concrete (cement, gravel, sand and water) are put into a drum. As the truck makes its way to a building site, the drum spins round, mixing the ingredients together. This *CIFA ENERGYA* mixer can carry nine cubic metres of concrete — enough to fill about 45 baths!

ENERGY
The drum motor batteries are recharged when the truck is parked.

FANTASTIC ⑤

CIFA ENERGYA CONCRETE MIXER

⚙ **Length:** 9.3 metres

⚙ **Width:** 2.4 metres

⚙ **Weight:** 26 tonnes

⚙ **Drum capacity:** 9 cubic metres

⚙ **Number of wheels:** 8

BACK OUT
To deliver the concrete, the drum spins backwards. The concrete slides down the delivery chute at the rear.

MASSIVE

The *BELAZ 75710* is the world's largest DUMP TRUCK. It's truly massive. It carries more stuff in one go than ten big **articulated** road trucks!

This beast of a truck carries coal around open-cast **coal mines**. It's moved along by four powerful electric motors. The electricity for the motors comes from **generators** turned by two powerful diesel engines. The truck rolls along on eight enormous wheels.

BELAZ 75710 DUMP TRUCK

⚙ **Length:** 20.6 metres

⚙ **Height:** 8.2 metres

⚙ **Weight:** 350 tonnes

⚙ **Capacity:** 450 tonnes

⚙ **Top speed:** 64 kilometres per hour

HOP ON
The driver's cab is so high up that the driver has to climb a set of stairs to get to it!

LOSE THE LOAD
The truck's huge dump compartment tips up to dump its load. It's pushed up from underneath by powerful hydraulic rams.

TALL

Construction engineers call in one of these super-tall trucks when they need to lift something really heavy. It's a giant MOBILE CRANE that can reach high and wide.

A mobile crane drives to a construction site along normal roads. When it arrives, its **boom** extends, other parts fold out and it's transformed from truck to crane, ready for action. The boom can be made even longer by adding extensions. This crane is the *LIEBHERR LTM 11200–9.1*, one of the world's biggest.

BOOM!
When the crane is on the road, the sections of the boom slide neatly into each other.

STEADY
The crane has stabilisers to stop it from toppling over when it's at work. These are legs with large pads at the end.

FANTASTIC 5

LIEBHERR LTM 11200-9.1

⚙ **Length on road:** 20 metres

⚙ **Maximum boom length:** 100 metres

⚙ **Maximum load:** 1,200 tonnes

⚙ **Maximum lifting height:** 188 metres

⚙ **Longest reach:** 138 metres

BULLETPROOF

This is a High Mobility Multipurpose Wheeled Vehicle, or HMMWV. Many soldiers simply call it a 'Humvee'.

A Humvee is a lightweight MILITARY TRUCK. It has four-wheel drive and rugged tyres, so it can drive off-road as well as on standard roads. This truck can fight equally well in cold and muddy conditions and in roasting desert heat. **Armour** protects the crew inside from attack. This Humvee version is called the *M1167*. It has an anti-tank missile launcher on its roof.

FANTASTIC

5

M1167 SERIES HMMWV

⚙ **Length:** 4.9 metres

⚙ **Weight:** 5.2–5.9 tonnes

⚙ **Top speed:** 113 kilometres per hour

⚙ **Range:** 402 kilometres

⚙ **Produced for:** US military, among others

WADE IN
This troop carrier version of the Humvee can drive through water up to 1.5 metres deep.

LIFTED UP
Humvees are often transported above the battlefield slung under a heavy-lift military helicopter.

SMOOTH

Huge, sleek GOODS TRUCKS like this rumble along highways of the world carrying all sorts of stuff from city to city, town to town and factory to shop.

The front part of this truck is known as the tractor. The tractor can pull any trailer, including a box trailer, flatbed trailer or a tanker trailer. The *DAF XF EURO 6* boasts bunk beds in the back of the cab, a powerful six-cylinder engine, 12 gears and super-bright **LED** headlights.

AIR LINES
Most trucks have air-powered brakes. Air goes to the trailer's brakes through hoses called air lines.

STREAMLINED
The body is curved and smooth, which allows air to flow around it easily as the truck speeds along.

FANTASTIC

5

DAF XF EURO 6

- ⚙ **Length:** 7.6 metres (up to 18.75 metres including trailer)
- ⚙ **Width:** 2.5 metres
- ⚙ **Weight:** 9.3 tonnes
- ⚙ **Maximum load when towing:** 40–60 tonnes
- ⚙ **Engine capacity:** 13 litres

SPEEDY

This RACING TRUCK has one job — to go fast! It blasts along with a deafening roar in a flurry of flames, heat and smoke. It's the world's fastest jet-powered truck.

Called *SHOCKWAVE*, this truck is a semi-trailer (the front part of an articulated truck) with three powerful **jet engines** bolted on the back. The engines are taken from old US Navy T2 Buckeye fighter planes. Shockwave spends its time entertaining crowds by appearing at **drag-racing** events, and by racing aircraft down runways at airshows.

FANTASTIC

5

SHOCKWAVE

- ⚙ **Weight:** 4 tonnes
- ⚙ **Engines:** 3 x jet engines
- ⚙ **Engine power:** 22,370 **kilowatts**
- ⚙ **Top speed:** 605 kilometres per hour
- ⚙ **Fuel capacity:** 720 litres

WINGS AND FINS

Two upright fins keep the truck going straight as it hurtles along. The wing pushes the wheels down onto the track to improve the tyres' grip.

MORE POWER

The jet engines have afterburners that squirt fuel into the hot exhaust gases. This doubles the engine power.

TEN MORE COOL FACTS

MONSTROUS: *Bigfoot* was one of the first monster trucks. Dave Chandler, the man who built Bigfoot, invented the sport of car crushing.

SHINY: The *Kenworth W900L* can pull a massive load. Together, the truck and its trailer may weigh more than 90 tonnes!

FLOATING: Twelve **Armoured Amphibious Assault Bridges (AAABs)** can be joined side by side to make a 150-metre-long floating bridge.

SLOW: The drivers of the *Alma transporters* sometimes have to wear oxygen masks because of the thin air at 5,000 metres above sea level, where they work.

HEAVY: The *Energya concrete mixer* has a kinetic energy recovery system (KERS). When the mixer slows down, some energy goes into the battery. KERS was first used on racing cars.

MASSIVE: When it's full of rubble, the *Belaz 75710* dump truck weighs more than 800 tonnes. That's as much as a fully loaded Airbus A380 airliner!

TALL: The *Liebherr LTM 11200-9.1* has a very long reach. If the crane were set up at one end of a football pitch, it could lift a small truck at the other end of the pitch into the air!

BULLETPROOF: The United States Army, Marines, Navy and other forces have more than 230,000 *Humvees* altogether! The trucks work as troop carriers, cargo carriers and ambulances.

SMOOTH: The engine of a *DAF XF Euro 6* is designed to last for 1.6 million kilometres before wearing out. That's the same distance as 40 times around the world!

SPEEDY: With its three jet engines, the *Shockwave* jet truck can accelerate very fast. From a standing start it covers 400 metres in under seven seconds, faster than the fastest sports cars!

STACK UP THOSE STATS!

Here are the ten cool machines with all their stats and a few more. Which machine is your favourite?

	Summit Racing Equipment Bigfoot	Kenworth W900L Studio Sleeper	Armoured Amphibious Assault Bridge	Alma Transporter	CIFA Energya Concrete Mixer	
Length	6 metres	8.8 metres	13 metres	20 metres	9.3 metres	
Width			3.5 metres	10 metres	2.4 metres	
Height			4.1 metres		8.2 metres	
Weight	5 tonnes		36 tonnes	130 tonnes	26 tonnes	
Engine capacity	9.3 litres	9 to 16 litres				
Carrying capacity					9 cubic metres	
Engine type and power	Methanol	Diesel	Diesel (522 hp)	2 x diesel (700 hp)		
Fuel capacity						
Top speed			50 kph (land) 10 kph (water)	20 kph	64 kph	
Number of gears		10–18				

Alma is the slowest truck on land.

QUIZ

1 What does Bigfoot crush under its wheels?

2 Which big truck has a sleeping compartment?

3 Which truck can turn into a bridge and a ferry?

4 How high do the Alma Transporters go?

5 Which machine uses electricity for mixing?

Belaz 75710	Liebherr LTM 11200–9.1	M1167 Series HMMWV	DAF XF Euro 6	Shockwave Jet Truck
20.6 metres	20 metres	4.5 metres	7.6 metres	
		2.16 metres	2.5 metres	
8.2 metres	188 metres	1.83 metres		
350 tonnes		5.2–5.9 tonnes	9.3 tonnes	4 tonnes
			13 litres	
450 tonnes	1,200 tonnes		40–60 tonnes	
2 x diesel (2,300 hp)	Diesel	Diesel (190 hp)	Diesel (412–510 hp)	3 x jet engines (22,370 kilowatts)
				720 litres
64 kph	113 kph			605 kph

Belaz is the heaviest truck.

Shockwave Is the fastest truck.

kph = kilometres per hour   lpm = litres per minute   hp = horsepower

7 Which truck has stabilising feet to stop it toppling over?

9 What is the front part of the DAF XF Euro 6 called?

10 Which truck has engines from a fighter plane?

6 How much coal can the Belaz 75710 carry?

8 Which truck is often carried by a helicopter?

GLOSSARY

amphibious something at home in water and on land

armour strong plates that protect a vehicle from bullets and explosions

articulated can bend in the middle

boom a long pole

cab the place where the driver sits

capacity space inside an engine, or the space inside the body of a truck

coal mine a place where coal is dug out of the ground

concrete material made from sand, gravel, cement and water mixed together, which sets hard after a few hours

drag racing a racing event where two vehicles race side by side along a short track

gears one of a set of cogs inside an engine that makes a machine move faster or slower, depending on which gear is chosen

generator a device that makes electricity from spinning movement

hybrid made up of two different things combined together

hydraulic ram a device that makes a push or a pull, a bit like a mechanical muscle

jet engine an engine that makes a fast-moving stream of hot gas

kilowatt unit of power, or how much energy an engine produces every second

Further Information

WEBSITES:

http://bigfoot4x4.com
All about the Bigfoot monster trucks, with plenty of photographs.

http://www.kenworth.com
Information about Kenworth trucks, including the famous W900L model.

https://www.liebherr.com
The Liebherr website. Click on 'Mobile and Crawler Cranes' to find information about Liebherr's huge cranes.

BOOKS
Mega Machines: Monster Trucks
by Amanda Askew
(QEB)
Ripley's Mighty Machines by Ian Graham
(Ripley)

Machines at Work: Trucks by Clive Gifford
(Wayland)

PLACES TO VISIT
British Commercial Vehicle Museum
This museum has many old trucks, including steam trucks.
http://www.britishcommercialvehiclemuseum.com

Santa Pod Raceway
Santa Pod is home to many motor racing events, including monster truck and truck racing shows.
http://www.santapod.co.uk

LED short for light emiting diode; a type of lightbulb

military to do with the army, navy, airforce or other armed forces

power steering system that helps a driver to steer

quarry a place where stone is dug out of the ground

suspension set of springs that let the wheels of a truck move up and down as the truck goes over bumps

telescope dish huge dish that collects radio waves coming from space so that astronomers can study the waves

water jets powerful jets of water that come from the hull of a boat to make it move along

INDEX

QUIZ ANSWERS
1 Bigfoot crushes cars.
2 The Kenworth W900L Studio Sleeper has a sleeping compartment.
3 The Armoured Amphibious Assault Bridge turns into a bridge or a ferry.
4 The Alma Transporters work at up to 5,000 metres above sea level.
5 The CIFA Energya Concrete Mixer has batteries to power its mixing drum.
6 The Belaz 75710 can carry 450 tonnes of coal.
7 The Liebherr LTM 11200–9.1 mobile crane has stabilising feet.
8 The M1167 Series HMMWV is often carried around a battlefield by helicopter.
9 It is called a tractor.
10 The Shockwave Jet Truck has three jet engines from a fighter plane.